Original title:
From Sprout to Shout

Copyright © 2025 Creative Arts Management OÜ
All rights reserved.

Author: Seraphina Caldwell
ISBN HARDBACK: 978-1-80566-600-4
ISBN PAPERBACK: 978-1-80566-885-5

Shades of Expression

A seedling dreams of heights so grand,
 Yet finds itself in garden land.
With worms as friends, it starts to share,
Some wiggly tales that make folks stare.

The sun shines bright, it raises cheer,
But soil's quirks bring laughter near.
 In whispers soft, the petals plot,
 To giggle loud and tie the knot.

The Crescendo of Growth

Little sprouts in row they stand,
Making plans, oh, isn't it grand?
They stretch and sway, in gentle breeze,
Declaring, 'We're the masters of ease!'

A bee buzzes past, a jester bold,
"Why grow up fast when young can be gold?"
They chuckle short, they laughter sprout,
Hoping to tickle all doubts out.

Rhapsody of Flora

In a garden lively, dance they do,
With petals and leaves, a bright hullabaloo.
The daisies tell jokes, the rose sings notes,
While dandelions wear funny coats.

Each plant a star in joy's parade,
Giggling in sun, never afraid.
"Life's a riot!" they all exclaim,
As blooms erupt and play the game.

Flourish in Freedom

No chains of weeds, no heavy ties,
Just laughter under open skies.
The ivy whispers jokes, quite sly,
While sunflowers shout, "Let's reach the sky!"

With every sprout, a giggle grows,
In nature's hands, their fun just flows.
Growing wild, they laugh and cheer,
Flourishing without a care or fear.

The Crescendo of Life Unfolding

In a garden, gnomes do dance,
With flowers wearing polka pants.
Bees buzz loud, a crazy choir,
While veggies dream of playing higher.

A potato juggles root and soil,
A carrot's joke makes laughter boil.
As sunlight tickles leaves so green,
Life's a show, oh what a scene!

Worms in bowties slide and twist,
Singing songs that can't be missed.
Buds pop out, what a surprise,
With funny faces, how they rise!

Nature's antics, a grand display,
In the garden, let's laugh all day!
From tiny seeds to plants that shout,
We're all in this wild dance, no doubt!

Radiant Blossoms and Boisterous Tales

The daisies gossip, so it seems,
While sunflowers play at counting dreams.
The tulips sway in colorful ranks,
Exchanging giggles, giving thanks.

A bumblebee wears a captain's cap,
Hitching a ride on a ladybug's lap.
Squirrels chat in their acorn suits,
While mushrooms plot their sneaky roots.

The rocks chuckle, the soil hums,
As a worm rolls by, tapping drums.
What wild tales the seedlings shout,
As the wind dances and twirls about!

Life's a carnival, bright and loud,
A parade of colors, a merry crowd!
The blossoms know just how to play,
In nature's laughter, we find our way!

A Silhouette of Silent Growth

In shadowed corners, seedlings woo,
They dream of growing tall and blue.
Underground whispers start to rise,
As tiny roots tell silly lies.

A sprig of thyme declares a play,
While radishes promote ballet.
The lettuce rolls away to hide,
As carrots peek out, filled with pride.

Crickets chuckle, sowbugs sway,
In this quiet green cabaret.
Each blossom bursts in crazy style,
With petals dancing, all the while!

Don't disturb the artful hush,
As buds are born with a joyful rush.
Nature grows in sly delight,
In playful shadows, out of sight!

The Roar of Nature's Fertility

With every seed a joke is told,
As pumpkins dream of being bold.
The violets hum a catchy tune,
While daisies wear a bright balloon.

The garden's wild, it swings and sways,
A berry sings of sunny days.
A cabbage giggles, rolling round,
As nature's laughter fills the ground.

The trees share whispers high and low,
While sprouts throw confetti in the flow.
Life's a roar of fun-filled cheer,
With nature's play, let's all draw near!

From tiny seeds to glory grand,
In this comedy, we all stand.
Join the leafy laugh parade,
Where every sprout has fun displayed!

Hushed Beginnings

In a garden where whispers reside,
Seeds chuckle, they can't hide.
Water dances, sun grins wide,
They sprout dreams, with joy inside.

Worms throw parties underground,
Mice on stilts prance around.
Quietly, laughter can be found,
In the soil where joy is crowned.

Tiny sprouts in silent play,
Buds giggle at the break of day.
Raising leaves in a grand ballet,
Nature's jesters on display.

The Language of Blooms

Petals gossip in soft hues,
Roses snicker, they share news.
Daisies wink at friendly views,
While tulips strike a pose, it's true!

Their colors chat in vibrant flair,
Sunflowers boast, "There's none to compare!"
Lilies flip a graceful hair,
While daisies scatter laughter in the air.

In this realm of leafy cheer,
Beetles buzz with tales to hear.
Nature's stand-up, no need to leer,
Every bloom holds joy quite near.

Flourishing in Silence

A shy sprout peeks from the ground,
Not a whisper, not a sound.
Yet beneath, the fun is found,
Worms in tuxedos spin around.

Roots chuckle at the stillness here,
While leaves share a nervous cheer.
In the stillness, they make it clear,
Joy is waiting, ever near.

With each rise, they bloom more bold,
Flaunting stories yet untold.
In their world, it's pure gold,
Laughter in green, joy uncontrolled.

The Roar of Colors

From greens to reds, a vibrant shout,
Colors giggle, dancing about.
Each hue loud, with laughter stout,
In petals' cheeks, no room for doubt.

Oranges sing with a playful sting,
Purples twirl, as if on a swing.
Every shade has a song to bring,
In their revelry, the flowers fling.

From violets soft to blues so deep,
Colors rally, they never sleep.
With every swirl, secrets they keep,
In the garden where joy takes a leap.

The Opus of the Orchard

In the orchard, a pear took a leap,
Said to an apple, "I have secrets to keep!"
The fruit laughed so hard, they rolled on the ground,
As cherries confided, "We can't make a sound!"

When the sun set low, the shadows would dance,
A grape tried to sing, but it looked like a trance!
The lemons all snickered, their zesty delight,
"Keep it down, we're citrus!" they yelled with a bite.

Ferns in the Breeze

Ferns swayed like dancers, all lost in the flow,
Whispering secrets that nobody knows.
A dandelion giggled, blowing seeds all around,
"I'm not just a weed, I'm the queen of the ground!"

The daisies chimed in, their charm was a spell,
"Let's throw a parade; oh, wouldn't it swell?"
But the ferns just kept dancing, with joy in their veins,
While the tulips rolled eyes at their fanciful claims.

The Rhapsody of Roots

Roots tangled and wrestling beneath the soft earth,
Claiming their spot, oh what a bizarre birth!
One root said to another, "Let's start a band!
With carrots on drums and a sapling so grand!"

But when they dug deep, they each fell asleep,
Snoozing away in this underground heap.
Worms giggled and teased, "Look who's missing the fun!"
They took up their spots, under moonlight they spun!

Celebrating Nature's Voice

In the meadow, a bug tried to sing out a tune,
With a pitch so off-key, it startled the moon.
Grasshoppers laughed, doing flips through the air,
While a sleepy old turtle just soaked in the flair.

The daisies applauded with petals so bright,
"Encore!" they all cried, under soft candlelight.
"Let's gather and party, let's dance 'til we drop!"
While the wind played the harp, and the branches would bop.

Rebirth in Every Green Awakening

In the soil, a party begins,
Tiny seeds with cheeky grins.
They wiggle and jiggle, dance all night,
Breaking ground, oh what a sight!

Sunshine tickles, rain gives a cheer,
Buds burst forth, no room for fear.
A sprout in a hat, how absurd!
Who knew plants could be so stirred?

Leafy arms waving in the breeze,
Here comes the worm, ready to tease.
"Let's grow big, let's touch the sky!"
Together they giggle, oh my, oh my!

Nature's show, a rambunctious spree,
Green confetti tossed wild and free.
With every inch, they declare with glee,
"We're the best buds, just wait and see!"

The Anthem of Life in Bloom.

A bud broke loose, it had some flair,
With pollen dreams flying through the air.
It sang a tune, oh what a blast,
"Blooming season, we're having a fast!"

Flowers pop with colors bright,
Bees buzz in with pure delight.
"Dance with me!" the petals yell,
A joyful ruckus, ringing bell!

Creepy crawlies join the fun,
Ladybugs and ants on the run.
"Let's make a garden, cool and grand,
With every sprout, we'll make a band!"

Roots tap-dance beneath the earth,
While breezes carry hints of mirth.
Together, they form a joyful choir,
Singing praises to their leafy empire!

Awakening in the Garden

One sunny morn, the garden yawns,
"All right, who left these silly prawns?"
Tiny shoots, with laughter bright,
Stretching arms in morning light.

Butterflies land with a fluttering spin,
"What's this party? Shall we begin?"
A daisy declared, "Join our parade!"
While dandelions threw a joyful charade.

Crickets chirp in stylish shoes,
"Don't be shy, we know the moves!"
With roots entwined, they join the dance,
Each leaf twirling in a happy trance.

The garden bustles, a wild affair,
With giggles floating through the air.
Nature's jesters, dressed in green,
Creating laughter like you've never seen!

The Whisper of Leaves

The leaves conspire in a hushed delight,
"Did you hear that? The sun is bright!"
They sway and giggle in the warm embrace,
"Come join the dance, it's time to race!"

With rustles and whispers, they share their dreams,
"Let's catch the breeze, and hear the streams!"
A light breeze passes, tickling their toes,
"Who knew life could be filled with prose?"

A crafty squirrel joins the spree,
"Let's scale the branches, climb with glee!"
And off they went, as swift as a wink,
Laughing and playing, they rarely think.

Leaves giggle sweetly, a playful crowd,
"Join in our laughter, it's fun, it's loud!"
In the heart of nature, where joy can't cease,
Each fluttering leaf finds its inner peace!

The Song of Sprigs

In the garden, leaves do dance,
Swaying swiftly in a prance.
Grasshoppers join with their own beat,
Chirping tunes beneath our feet.

Tiny buds begin to poke,
Tickled by a gentle joke.
A sunflower laughs, a petal twirls,
As daisies giggle, swaying girls.

With every drop of morning dew,
The plants sing out, a lively crew.
Rabbits hop, and squirrels tease,
While roots are tickled by the breeze.

A bumblebee buzzes with glee,
Making friends with a bumble tree.
In this garden, life's a song,
Join the fun; you can't go wrong!

The Harmonies of Blooming

Petals burst in rainbow hues,
Nature's giggles, a joyful muse.
Bees are buzzing, full of cheer,
While flowers whisper, "Come on, dear!"

A flower yawns, stretches wide,
Leaves around it fit and glide.
The tulips wink, a sneaky flinch,
As butterflies dance, giving a pinch.

Every blossom spreads a grin,
Shaking off the morning's din.
Trees sway, telling stories bold,
Of blooming dreams that never grow old.

In this patch of silly delight,
Life's a festival, shining bright.
Join the chorus, sing it loud,
For in this garden, we're all proud!

The Dawn of Decibels

Morning breaks, the sun says hi,
A chorus starts—oh me, oh my!
The crickets chirp, a catchy beat,
While roosters cluck, a rhythmic tweet.

Vines wrap around in a playful race,
Yelling, "Catch me, if you can place!"
Hilarity blooms from roots so deep,
As laughter echoes, waking from sleep.

Caterpillars rock in the sun,
Transforming plans—they're so much fun!
A leaf drops down with a silly plop,
While mushrooms jump and never stop.

The morning turns to one big laugh,
As grasshoppers break into a half.
With every chirp and rustling leaf,
The dawn of sound is our belief!

Blooming Rebellion

In a garden of giggles and grins,
A riot of color where fun begins.
Petals protest, "We'll paint the sky!"
While stubborn weeds dream of flying high.

The tomatoes cheer in juicy red,
"Join us, friends! Let's paint the shed!"
A root declares, "No more dirt, no way!"
As herbs plot fun in the bright bouquet.

The carrots march with tops held high,
Making noise, oh my, oh my!
Radishes join with a spicy scent,
Creating chaos, wherever they went.

The flowers laugh, with mischief fair,
Waving banners in the air.
A blooming revolution takes a stand,
With every sprout, we rule this land!

The Unveiling of Nature's Canvas

In the garden, blooms do giggle,
Petals dance, they twist and wiggle.
Sunshine whispers, clouds just tease,
Bees in hats, buzzing with ease.

Nature's palette splashes bright,
Caterpillars take a flight.
Daffodils in polka dots,
Tulips prance in silly spots.

Ladybugs wear spots with pride,
While snails take their time to slide.
Every critter's got a role,
In this show, it's quite the stroll.

Laughter bubbles in the breeze,
With flowers trying to appease.
Garden gnomes share a wink,
In this painted world, we think.

Flourish and Flourish Again

Watch me stretch, I'm full of glee,
Growing tall like I'm a tree.
Bending low for sun's embrace,
Every day is a silly race.

Roots beneath, they wiggle free,
Dancing deep, oh can't you see?
Leaves throw parties up above,
Fluttering like they're in love.

Seeds are giggling in the dirt,
Wiggling worms wear little skirts.
Each new sprout takes on the stage,
Growing up with such wild rage.

Back and forth, the weeds are sly,
Catching raindrops as they fly.
Nature's jesters, full of cheer,
Join the dance, come on, my dear!

The Symphony of Roots and Leaves

Roots play bass, they thump and thud,
Leaves keep time with a leafy flood.
Breezes blow a tune so sweet,
While bugs tap dance on little feet.

In this orchestra, all unite,
With sun as conductor, oh so bright.
Frogs croak bass, birds whistle high,
While daisies sway and butterflies fly.

Chorus of crickets starts to sing,
As blossoms nod in a lively ring.
Nature hums a merry song,
Where everything feels so very wrong.

Listen close, it's a funny show,
As each plant puts on a glow.
Underneath, where roots dig deep,
Laughter blooms while the world sleeps.

Tales of the Sprouting Life

Once a seed, as tiny as can be,
Dreamed of sunlight, oh what glee!
Pushed through soil, it took its chance,
Underneath, the worms did dance.

A ladybug gave it a cheer,
"Grow up big, my friend, don't fear!"
With a stretch, the sprout took flight,
Reaching up towards stars so bright.

Flowers bloomed with laughter loud,
Sharing stories in a crowd.
Bumblebees wrote the town's best tale,
Of leaves in hats, it couldn't fail.

In this garden, fun's the key,
Every sprout is wild and free.
Laughter echoes, day and night,
In nature's fun, there's pure delight.

Cadence of the Field

In the meadow, weeds take a dance,
Strutting their stuff without a chance.
Sunflowers whisper, 'Look at us sway!'
While grumpy old weeds just curse the day.

Bumblebees buzz with a comedic hum,
Try to outsmart a nearby plum.
Grasshoppers leap like they own the place,
But trip on a twig, oh what a face!

The daisies giggle, so wild and free,
Chasing each other like a wobbly bee.
Ants march by in a disciplined line,
But lose their way, thinking it's sunshine!

A scarecrow grins, his eyes full of glee,
Watching the chaos from his seat by the tree.
"Life's a joke," he calls, while crows take flight,
And the whole field bursts into laughter that night.

Nature's Declaration

Leaves debate on what shade is best,
While squirrels argue about their next quest.
Wind whispers jokes with a giggly cheer,
Tickling the flowers, 'Come join us here!'

The river chuckles, splashing with flair,
As frogs croak loudly, without a care.
Sunshine winks, casting playful light,
On bugs that tango, what a silly sight!

Rocky cliffs boast of wisdom and age,
But tumble a little, quite off their stage.
Mossy carpets, green and round,
Muffle the giggles beneath the ground.

Dancing daisies roll their eyes and sing,
"Life's a jest, and we're the bling!"
So nature's here, with laughter so bright,
In a world where giggles take flight.

Rooted Resonance

In cool, damp soil, roots wrestle with glee,
Bouncing around like a tight-knit family.
Little sprouts tease, 'You think you're the best?'
But flowers just laugh, 'We'll put you to rest!'

Rain giggles down, makes puddles for fools,
As worms wiggle by, breaking all rules.
'Hey there, sunbeam, shine just a bit!',
Said a timid bulb, excited to sit.

Wind carries whispers, tickling the grass,
While napping daisies let hours pass.
With roots all entwined, secrets are shared,
Oh, the fun in the garden, so joyfully bared.

Pumpkins roll in, thinking they're kings,
'We'll take the contest for the biggest bling!'
And with all this humor, the earth spins 'round,
In a rooted resonance, laughter is found.

A Flourishing Tale

Once there was a sprout, with dreams so grand,
Wished to be a flower, in a wondrous land.
"Look at me grow!" it said with delight,
But worms whispered back, "You're in for a fright!"

The sunbeam chuckled, sharing rays with fun,
"Keep reaching high, soon you'll be number one!"
As petals unfurl, they play peek-a-boo,
While bees buzzed in, ready for brew.

Then came a storm, with thunderous glee,
But the sprout just laughed, "You can't bother me!"
Rain danced around, with barrels of cheer,
While the roots sang out, "We've nothing to fear!"

At last, it bloomed, in colors so bright,
And laughter echoed, a marvelous sight.
Through trials and tales, it learned to be bold,
In nature's garden, a legend retold.

Dialogue of the Flowers

In the garden, blooms debate,
Petals in a frenzied state.
'Why do bees buzz all around?'
'They think we wear the finest gown!'

Roses argue, daffodils tease,
'I'm the prettiest, if you please!'
Tulips roll their eyes in glee,
'Petal fights, oh let it be!'

Songs of the Soil

The earth hums a silly tune,
Worms dance beneath the silver moon.
'Why dig deep when you can play?'
'Soil parties last all day!'

Grayscale roots tap and clap,
Chasing joy in a joyful nap.
'We're all the rage, you see,
In this dirt, we're fancy-free!'

Flourishing Fragments

Petals flutter like tiny flags,
With tiny jokes that make us gag.
'Can't touch this, I'm a daisy!'
'Oh really? Think you're so crazy!'

Sunflowers dance in the breeze,
Throwing shade like they're in fees.
But who's the tallest in the plot?
'Guess it's me, or maybe not!'

Blossoms Speak

Blossoms gossip, petals prance,
Sharing secrets in a chance.
'Heard the tulip's gone on strike!'
'What for? Not enough sunlight!'

Lilies giggle, violets grin,
'Is it spring or a flower sin?'
Every bloom with tales to tell,
Makes the garden ring like a bell!

The Vibrant Awakening

In the garden, seeds do mix,
Tiny sprouts play little tricks.
They wiggle then they shake,
Unfurling leaves, oh what a break!

Sunshine beams, the bugs all cheer,
Dancing close, they spread the cheer.
The daisies laugh, the tulips tease,
While bumblebees buzz with ease.

Chickens cluck in comical spree,
As veggie tales grow wild and free.
Radishes in riot, carrots in bloom,
They lean in close, make room, make room!

Fruits take a tumble, what a sight,
Melons roll down, oh what a fright!
Laughter echoes through the patch,
Nature's jest, a wiggling match!

Whispers in the Wind

Leaves whisper secrets, soft and clear,
They giggle beneath the rolling sphere.
Swaying gently, in humorous spins,
Wiggling tales of where it begins.

A squirrel struts with nuts to show,
While leaping frogs join in the flow.
Chirping birds crack jokes on high,
Making clouds giggle in the sky.

Breezes tickle the flowers' petals,
As oddball blooms wear sunny medals.
Hiccups from a clumsy bee,
Spread chuckles 'round the leafy spree.

When rain drops down, it starts a game,
Puddles form, and splashes claim.
The earth erupts in fitting mirth,
A rollicking joy, a heavenly birth!

The Clamor of Color

Colors clash in vibrant delight,
A rainbow parade, oh what a sight!
Purple giggles, orange sways,
While greens and blues dance in a haze.

Pansies prank with silly grins,
As marigolds tease, the laughter spins.
The tulips twirl in high and low,
A dizzying disco, what a show!

Dandelions float, like fluffy lies,
Tumbling down from sunny skies.
They tickle the toes of passing friends,
With whimsical wishes that never ends.

The corn stalks sway and shout with glee,
Join the merry garden jubilee!
It's a feast of fun, a glorious spree,
In a world where laughter sets us free!

Cadence of the Canopy

High in the trees, the branches sway,
Barking jokes in the light of day.
Monkeys mimic with silly faces,
Creating laughter in leafy places.

Squirrels chatter with raspy calls,
As curious owls peek from their halls.
Wobbly walkers, they tumble and hop,
Flipping and flopping, they never stop!

Breezes croon through the emerald crowd,
Filling the air with whispers loud.
Sunbeams dance on the forest floor,
A joyful beat we can't ignore.

Rustling leaves join the comical round,
Nature's rhythm, a jolly sound.
With each rustle, a chuckle rings,
The canopy claps as the wildlife sings!

Symphonies of Nature's Awakening

In the garden, laughter blooms,
Worms are wiggling to their tunes.
Bees wear hats, they dance and swing,
Nature's band is ready to sing.

The daisies hold a flower show,
While butterflies flit to and fro.
A rose pipes up with a bold joke,
And nearby, a tulip starts to croak.

Swaying blades of grass all sway,
As ants compete in a three-legged relay.
The sun beams down, a spotlight bright,
On this grand performance, pure delight.

Laughter echoes in the trees,
As squirrels giggle in the breeze.
A pine cone wears a crown of leaves,
Nature's circus never deceives.

Murmurs Beneath the Surface

In the soil, whispers share,
Roots are gossiping with flair.
Worms are plotting little schemes,
Dreaming big with leafy dreams.

A pebble claims it's quite the sage,
As grass proposes a silly wage.
Fungi flip through gossip rags,
Spreading tales of snails with flag wag.

Underneath the ground, they jest,
Sharing snacks, they feast the best.
A hidden world, a furry party,
Where every creature feels so smarty.

But when a raindrop starts to fall,
They scramble quick, it's a funnel call.
The merry mud makes quite the splash,
As all the seedlings come in a dash.

Voices of the Rising Flora

Petals yawn and stretch awake,
The morning sun makes flowers quake.
A sunflower points and shouts out loud,
'Look at me, I'm quite the proud!'

Tulips giggle in their rows,
As daisies tell jokes, everyone knows.
A lily boasts of its lovely scent,
While dandelions blow seeds that went.

In whispers soft, they share their dreams,
Of garden parties and soft sunbeams.
With every breeze, they sway and hum,
In a chorus of joy, their voices strum.

An earthquake makes a flower stumble,
And all unite in laughter's rumble.
A bloom declares, "Let's have a game!"
And thus, they play, without any shame.

Journey of the Budding Dreams

Little seeds packed tight in a bag,
One whispered, 'Don't you dare brag!'
A sprout stood tall and said with glee,
'Just wait for me, I'll be a tree!'

Out they popped, in sunlight's grace,
A clumsy dance, a leafy race.
With every stretch, they shout aloud,
'Look at us, we're nature's crowd!'

A fallen branch, a curious sight,
Said, 'Gather round, let's share tonight!'
They swapped their stories, time well spent,
Filled with giggles, their laughter bent.

But when the rain began to pour,
They jumped around, they loved it more!
With puddles made, they jumped and splashed,
Budding dreams in moments, made a splash.

Nature's Narrative

In the garden, quite a sight,
Worms wear jackets, pure delight!
Beetles throwing little balls,
Laughing in the leafy halls.

Bumblebees in tuxedo stripes,
Practicing for buzzing gripes,
Dancing daisies, twirling fast,
Forgetting winter's chilly blast.

Squirrels in a nutty race,
Chasing tails in a quick pace,
While mushrooms play a secret tune,
Underneath the laughing moon.

Nature's cast, a vibrant show,
Where all the oddballs seem to glow,
Tune in close, enjoy the cheer,
A giggle fest each time of year.

Revelry in Bloom

Tulips throwing quite a bash,
Daisies dressed in splendid sash,
They sip on nectar, share a laugh,
While violets take a silly half.

Marigolds hosting games galore,
Petunias dance around the floor,
Gardens filled with jovial jest,
Nature's party, simply the best!

Butterflies in wild disguise,
Pretend to be the birds that fly,
While ladybugs play hide and seek,
With bumblebees who say, "Not weak!"

Come join the fun, the blooms invite,
In laughter, everything feels right,
A riot of color, sight and sound,
Where giggles of nature can be found.

Voices of Vigor

Funny frogs with booming croaks,
Crackling jokes like silly folks,
Fluffy clouds join in the jest,
As leaves clap hands in happy zest.

The trees are whispering sweet rhymes,
Birds drop puns from lofty climbs,
Sunshine giggles through the leaves,
While grasshoppers pull off pranks like thieves.

Chirping crickets serenade,
While weeds join in the grand parade,
Roses blush at jests so bright,
Their petals twitch with sheer delight.

Nature's band, a lively choir,
In every giggle, there's desire,
To sing out loud, come join the fun,
Where laughter dances, never done.

Silent Symphony

In the hush, a secret sprout,
Whispers of giggles dance about,
Buds tremble with a playful tease,
As the wind pipes up, "Just breathe!"

Rich roots underground, they snicker,
At the slowpoke flowers, feel the ticker,
As petals play a guessing game,
"Who's the brightest? Who's to blame?"

A snail in shades, he takes it slow,
While ants perform their circus show,
Dandelions puff and puff,
Making wishes, just enough!

In silence blooms a loud delight,
Nature's laughter, pure and bright,
A symphony without a sound,
Where jokes and joy abound!

Stages of the Green Serenade

In the garden, seeds awake,
Dancing with the morning shake.
Tiny leaves begin to grin,
Whispering tales of growth within.

Worms start to groove a little jig,
While bees buzz by, oh so big!
Sunshine spills like lemonade,
Nature laughs, and plans are made.

Roots twirl deep beneath the ground,
Unseen parties, never found!
A sprig of thyme shows off its flair,
While daisies tease with colors rare.

Then comes a bloom, bright and bold,
With stories of sunshine told.
A festival of colors proud,
Nature's laugh spills out loud!

Cadence of the Flora's Journey

Tiny seeds with dreams so grand,
Spin around in merry bands.
They stretch their limbs, oh what a sight,
Chasing clouds, playing with light.

Sprouts peek out with silly hats,
Hiding from the curious cats!
Fluttering leaves play hide and seek,
With chirpy birds that love to squeak.

A sunflower strikes a goofy pose,
While lilacs giggle, heavens knows!
Naughty vines play a cheeky game,
Bounding forth, they earn their fame.

Then blossoms burst, a colorful cheer,
Causing onlookers to draw near.
Nature laughs, with petals in tow,
In a bright parade, they steal the show!

The Unfolding of Nature's Heart

A seed once shy, starts to shout,
With a gleeful little sprout.
It wiggles and jigs in the sun,
Saying, "Oh, growth is so much fun!"

The grass gets jealous, starts to sway,
Singing along, day after day.
Petals flutter with no fear,
Blowing kisses to all, so dear.

Bumblebees join in with a buzz,
Chasing dreams, just because!
Bright tulips play dress-up with flair,
Twirling in the warm spring air.

And as the garden starts to glow,
With laughter high, and joy to flow.
Nature grins, a heart so bright,
In the dance of day and night!

The Flourishing Song of Tomorrow

Once a seed, now a leaf parade,
Marching forth, they're not afraid!
With a shimmy and a shake,
They tease the sun, oh for goodness' sake!

Roots are gossiping down below,
Sharing secrets we'll never know.
While daffodils in bluebird hats,
Dance with butterflies and chat!

Pansies sprouting with a wink,
Quipping jokes that make you think.
Nature's humor, sly and spry,
Leaves of laughter in the sky.

A jolly bud breaks forth with flair,
Spinning tales, so full of air.
And as the blooms sing loud and clear,
Tomorrow's song is always near!

Roars of Resilience

In a garden where veggies take a stand,
A carrot jokes, 'I'm the best in the land!'
With radishes giggling and let's not forget,
Our leafy greens dance, not a single regret.

Each sprout tells a tale of climbing high,
Tomatoes whisper secrets, oh so sly!
While beans try their best to twirl and twist,
Laughing at puns that simply can't be missed.

With sunlight's tickle and rain's warm cheer,
The plants throw a party, inviting all near,
Even the weeds, with their wild, winding ways,
Join in the laughter, turning workdays to plays.

So when you feel small and quite out of place,
Remember those sprouts sprouting dreams with grace,
For every shudder in nature's big show,
There's a roar of resilience, letting joy grow!

Wandering Wisps

In a field where dandelions dance and sway,
They giggle at bees who bumble and play.
A butterfly flutters, wearing a crown,
Wandering wisps, never wearing a frown.

Grass blades gossip about clouds passing by,
'Look at that shape! Is it a cupcake or pie?'
The sun winks down, making shadows that tease,
While crickets compose quite the melody breeze.

A sunflower stands tall, striking a pose,
While ants form a line, 'To the picnic!' it goes.
With nature's own laughter, they wriggle and shout,
In the heart of the wild, that's what it's about!

So let laughter grow, in fields and in woods,
For nature's a playground, in all of its hoods.
From flowers to flies, everyone's part,
In the funny old tale of a wandering heart!

Nature's Vivace

In the forest where trees wiggle with glee,
A squirrel steals snacks, as slick as can be.
While mushrooms giggle, dressed in shades bright,
Nature's vivace dances, oh what a sight!

A bear with a top hat performs with delight,
While birds sing operas, taking flight.
The wind plays a tune, a rustling refrain,
As flowers keep time, in this nature's domain.

With rhythm and laughter, the leaves start to sway,
Chasing the bugs, who just want to play.
Each moment's a laugh, a silly ballet,
In the heart of the wild, joy's here to stay!

So raise up your voices, both loud and well,
Let's join in the clamor, just listen and tell.
For in nature's grand show, the fun never fades,
In this playful, bright world, let's dance with cascades!

Glorious Growth

In the dirt where the wildflowers twirl,
A tiny seed dreams of being a girl.
With each little push, and the sun's warm glow,
What a glorious journey, watch how we grow!

The comical bugs parade on a leaf,
Playing tag, oh what a goofball relief!
While ladybugs laugh at the ants on the run,
In this crazy green world, oh it's so much fun!

Rabbits hop past with a flourish and flip,
Having picnics with friends, in a whimsy-filled trip.
The flowers are cheering, the grass sings along,
Nature's own choir, the perfect big song!

So sprinkle a laugh, let your heart bloom bright,
For growth is a giggle, a sheer pure delight.
In every small moment, there's joy to be found,
In the dance of the flowers, let laughter abound!

Blossom's Anthem

In a garden full of glee,
Petals dance like crazy bees,
A tulip twirled in bright pink shoes,
Singing songs of springtime blues.

A daffodil slipped on the dew,
Told a joke that just won't do,
The roses laughed, they're such a tease,
As daisies float on the light breeze.

The Chorus of Change

Oh, the sprout tried to sing a tune,
But tripped and fell beneath the moon,
The soil chuckled, worms in delight,
As the grasshopper hummed all night.

A caterpillar joined the show,
In a hat two sizes too low,
With a wobbly dance and grand ballet,
He slipped right into a worm buffet!

Melody in the Meadow

A bumblebee buzzed, all off-key,
Chased by ants in a wild spree,
The daisies swayed, what a view,
While sunbeams played hide and boo!

The clouds giggled, such friendly fluff,
As critters interacted, not tough,
With grass tickling their little feet,
They danced around to the meadow's beat.

Unfurling Dreams

A tiny seed had big ideas,
To wear a crown, just not in fears,
It sprouted arms, not quite like those,
But waved at squirrels, struck funny poses.

With laughter echoing through the green,
The flowers formed a comedy scene,
Where every blossom, bold and bright,
Shouted joy 'til the stars gave light.

Voice of the Seedling

A tiny seed, I take the lead,
With dreams of soil and sunlight's need.
My roots wiggle, it's quite a sight,
Telling worms I'm ready for flight!

I sprout up high, with so much glee,
A leaf on my head, just wait and see.
The ants parade, my leafy crown,
While I think, 'Hey, I won't drown!'

The breeze laughs low as I twist and giggle,
Whispering secrets that make me wiggle.
I flex my stems, oh what a pose,
With nature's fashion show, I'm the only rose!

With sun's warm hug, I twist and shout,
"My leafy way is what it's all about!"
Who knew a sprout could have such fun?
It's not just growth, it's a leafy run!

Expressing Dawn

The sun peeks in, my morning cheer,
I stretch my leaves, feel the atmosphere.
A dance begins on dew-kissed ground,
The world wakes up to my silly sound!

With a wiggle here and a sway right there,
I flaunt my greens, with utmost flair.
The flowers giggle, oh what a sight,
As I chant, "Good day!" with all my might!

Birds join in, singing tunes so sweet,
While I sway gently, tapping my feet.
Together we joke, the sky so bright,
A chorus of joy at the morning light!

So, let's spread jests till the day is done,
A leafy party, oh what fun!
With every whisper and rustle of leaves,
We'll celebrate this joy, no one believes!

Echoes of Green

In this forest, whispers gleam,
A leafy chorus, a growing dream.
Rabbits hop, and squirrels tease,
While branches sway in the playful breeze.

"Oh, look at me!" the ferns declare,
"We're dressing up for the grand affair!"
But roots get tangled, and oh, what a fuss,
With every tug, we giggle and cuss!

The breeze steals laughs, so light, so merry,
As my petals flutter all bright and cherry.
With every turn, a new joke is spun,
In the world of green, we're all just fun!

So join the jive, sway slow then fast,
With echoing laughs, let's have a blast!
Beneath the sky, where dreams collide,
The forest's jokes are our leafy pride!

Rising to the Sun

With every dawn, I play my game,
Dancing up high, I make my name.
The sun beams down, and I take my stand,
Waving my arms, oh isn't this grand?

Butterflies flutter by with a grin,
"Join us, friend! Let the fun begin!"
I twist and twirl, so carefree,
"My leafiest moves are a sight to see!"

The grass below joins in the song,
As I leap, shout, and stretch along.
They cheer me on, "Go, leafy champ!"
While I bask bright in my green-clad lamp!

So up I rise, with zest and zeal,
In this garden realm, there's plenty to feel.
With every chuckle and leafy leap,
I'm shouting my joy, a promise I'll keep!

The Tale of Tendrils

In a garden where giggles grow,
Tendrils tickle, putting on a show.
They stretch and twist, what a sight,
A dance of green in morning light.

The beans have dreams of climbing high,
While squash plays tag, oh my oh my!
With snickers and chuckles, plants unite,
Creating a circus, pure delight.

The radishes wear tiny hats,
Jumping like silly acrobats.
Carrots wiggle, sharing jest,
In this garden, they're all the best!

But beware of the weedy vote,
They'll crash the party, not remote.
Yet laughter grows, a joyful sound,
In this quirky patch, fun abounds!

The Harmonious Harvest

In twilight's glow, the veggies sing,
A tune that makes the garden ring.
The tomatoes laugh, the peppers cheer,
A harvest jam, oh lend an ear!

The corn sings sweet, a jazzy tune,
While carrots groove beneath the moon.
Their leafy friends, they sway and sway,
A farmyard dance, hip-hip-hooray!

Zucchinis hold a concert bright,
With turnips playing drums at night.
They swish and swirl, the ground does quake,
A frolic fest, make no mistake!

With every laugh, a veggie grows,
In rhyming rows, the fun just flows.
So raise a toast to greens and gold,
In harmony, let tales be told!

The Flourishing Fugue

In a patch where giggles meet,
A fugue of flowers, oh so sweet!
Petals prance in colors bold,
A sight to see, a sight to hold.

Daisies duel with marigolds,
With tickling roots and stories told.
Chives chant rhymes, with garlic too,
Creating chaos, colorful brew!

Tiny bees join flitting fun,
Buzzing tunes beneath the sun.
They waltz on blooms, a joyous spree,
The garden's alive with glee!

As night descends, the stars will twirl,
While veggie hearts spin and whirl.
A flourished dance, forever growing,
In this land of laughter, glowing!

Raindrops and Resonance

Raindrops tap a funny beat,
On leaves that wiggle with their feat.
They laugh aloud, a splashy cheer,
As puddles form, oh dear, oh dear!

The peas pop up, with glee they shout,
As water's wonder spins about.
Radishes bounce in muddy shoes,
While peppers play, they never lose!

With every drop, the giggles swell,
A watery story, oh can you tell?
The garden's rhythm splashes wide,
As veggies dance, with none to hide!

The sun peeks out, a radiant grin,
While roots rejoice beneath the skin.
So raise a cheer for rain's embrace,
In droplets' joy, we find our place!

The Sound of Roots

Deep in the soil, where the worms play,
Roots dance to music, in a wobbly way.
One planted seed said, "Oh, how I long,
To break free and sing, in a rooty song!"

The beetles join in with a tap on the ground,
While the rocks start a beat that's wonderfully loud.
Earthworms are grooving, what a sight to behold,
Nature's own concert, funny and bold!

Do we hear the whispers when the leaves take flight?
Giggling softly, they soar to delight.
In the shade, the grass chortles, "Oh, what a tune!"
As the sun sneezes bright, under a big, silly moon.

Symphony of Growth

Tiny green sprouts, so eager to play,
Swaying and tipping, come join the ballet!
In the garden's great hall, they take to the stage,
With broccoli hats that make them feel sage!

Tomatoes twirl round, in red, shiny coats,
While peas in their pods sing notes like old goats.
A sunflower's solo, so tall and so grand,
With petals like trumpets, it takes a firm stand!

And let's not forget the clumsy old weeds,
Who dance like they're lost, but with innocent needs.
They trip on their roots, and the daisies all laugh,
As they tumble and roll like a comical calf.

A Journey of Leaves

A leaf set out one sunny day,
To find the best breeze, and soar away.
It flapped its edges, with a funny twist,
"I'm on my great journey, and you know what I've missed?"

It met a flower, all dressed up in style,
"Join me, dear friend, we'll dance for a while!"
But the flower just giggled and said with a grin,
"Sorry, my roots are tied up in a spin!"

Next came a bug, with a top hat so fine,
"Would you like to waltz, and sip some sweet brine?"
But when the leaf swayed, it lost its cool stance,
And landed in mud, oh what a mischance!

Beneath the Surface

Under the ground, where the critters all meet,
The moles throw a party, with worms as their beat.
They dig up the snacks, oh what a delight!
"Come join the fun, it's an underground night!"

The gophers are snickering, "Let's bring in some cake!"
While the roots start to wiggle, in a riotous shake.
"What's life without laughter?" the radish declares,
"Let's all toast to fun, and forget all our cares!"

But just as the fun reached a peak with a cheer,
A mole shouted, "Shh! There's a gardener near!"
The party went quiet, then burst into shouts,
Nature's funny whispers, escaping through sprouts!

www.ingramcontent.com/pod-product-compliance
Lightning Source LLC
Chambersburg PA
CBHW071813160426
43209CB00003B/73